ARRIVAL

Also by Cheryl Boyce-Taylor

Convincing the Body

Night When Moon Follows

Of Fire, Of Iron (as editor)

Raw Air

ARRIVAL

Poems

Cheryl Boyce-Taylor

TRIQUARTERLY BOOKS / NORTHWESTERN UNIVERSITY PRESS

EVANSTON, ILLINOIS

TriQuarterly Books
Northwestern University Press
www.nupress.northwestern.edu

Copyright © 2017 by Cheryl Boyce-Taylor. Published 2017 by TriQuarterly Books /
Northwestern University Press. All rights reserved.

Printed in the United States of America

10   9   8   7   6   5   4   3   2   1

ISBN 978-0-8101-3514-7 (paper)
ISBN 978-0-8101-3515-4 (e-book)

Cataloging-in-Publication Data are available from the Library of Congress.

The paper used in this publication meets the minimum requirements of the American
National Standard for Information Sciences—Permanence of Paper for Printed Library
Materials, ANSI Z39.48–1992.

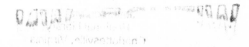

For my parents,
Eugenia Elma Boyce and Fitzroy Blackette

And in memory of my beloved son
Malik Boyce-Taylor (a.k.a. Phife Dawg)

She is crouched in small places trying to relearn her eyes
she wants to remember how joy lingers.
—cbt

Contents

Spell

Arrival

Acknowledgments

Poems in this collection have appeared previously in: *Adrienne*; *Calabash Literary Journal of Arts & Letters*; *NYU*; *Killins Review of Arts & Letters*; *PANK*; *Revolutionary Mothering: Love on the Front Lines*; *Prairie Schooner*; *The Mom Egg Review*; *To Be Left with the Body*; *APLA*. Special thanks to the editors.

Heartfelt gratitude to Parneshia Jones and the entire Northwestern family for honoring this collection.

To Desciana Swinger, my life partner and friend. Everything is possible with you.

Deepest gratitude to Aracelis Girmay for your close reading and strong edits on *ARRIVAL*. Bless those wise and beautiful eyes of yours.

Thanks to Kimiko Hahn and Kwame Dawes for your editing and guidance.

A huge shout out to my poet buddies who gave feedback on my poems or invited me to read: EJ Antonio; Cheryl Clarke; Anton Nimblett; Ed Toney; Roger Bonair-Agard; Steven G. Fullwood, Kathy Engel; Yesenia Montilla; JP Howard; Golda Solomon; Patricia Spears Jones; Bonnie Rose Marcus; Mariahadessa Ekere Tallie; Patrick Rosal; Rachel Eliza Griffiths; Lynne Procope. I miss you RH Douglas, my best friend and writing wife. You changed my life with your bright colors, sass, and Trini dialect.

Thank you to my many reading and writing communities: VONA; Cave Canem: Urban Word NYC; Louder Arts Project; Poets & Writers; The Wide Shore; The Glitter Pomegranate Reading Series; Calypso Muse; and Elma's Heart Circle.

To my family: This book would not be possible without my parents, Elma Eugenia Boyce and Fitzroy Blackette. Bless your heart, my beautiful son, Malik Boyce-Taylor. You are always next to me. I talk to you every day. Heartfelt thanks to that wise woman, Deisha Head Taylor, my daughter-in-law, and to David Armstrong, my grandson. To Russell Boyce and the Swinger, Clemmons-Larsson, and Boyd families. To Donna Lee Weber, Angela Holloway, and Patricia Starek. You hold me up always. Thank you.

RIDING THE WORLD

Wild Sorrel

—if dem chiren hit me today
I go hit dem back what about you cherylallison,
what you go do

praise Dara's dare and her spell of words
praise my swift backhand and the girl that fell
tearing her ass wide   praise father
who did not tell mother

praise my shy girl learning to be tough
praise the dust and the girl that rose
praise the chest that puffed to bursting—
the chest raised with new breasts tucked in blue bra
praise the new breasts

it was love not poverty that made my first homemade bra
Mammie and Tanty Verna's hands buzzed
with the Singer sewing machine
they singing along to Calypso

one sister stopped to snap her fingers
shake her tiny butt
one ran the tap water a little 'til it ran clear
the other made the limeade   drank it without ice

one wiggled to young Elvis
he the new blue-suede-shoe crooner
they black pony-tailed half-girls
bright red bindi in the middle of their foreheads
milk still warm in their green-mango breasts

a hip slung low beige piece of moon bright in her narrow dress
blue-corn silk ribbons holding breeze at bay
my Trinidad her red Ixora flush of dusk
her sugar-diabetes running wild

at nine the demon of menstrual cramps drummed all night
Mammie boiled wormgrass tea for pain
every Sunday bike rides   tears
castor oil straight   and orange soda for chaser

years later orange soda would soothe my monthly cramps
its taste reminded me of my childhood mangoes
its center jellied and damp
as an inner womb readying
my ivory bowl for twin boys

blessed with twins
one would stand before Oya
the other would clap and whirl spin words

one would hear river talking
the other would write it down
one would change the world
the other would leave it

from wind's beak once fell two seeds
one a bird the other a girl
turned wild sorrel tree.

I Name Gyal

I name gyal
I know who I am
braided gyal drinking cocoa tea

hands rooted in pigeon peas
my home name is gyal
gyal whey yuh going in yuh Sunday best dress

gyal yuh still on dat phone
gyal back chat does get yuh back slap

young gyal make up yuh bed please
it eh ha no maid living here yuh know
yes Mammie

gyal yuh must soak de fruit
and currents in rum bout three
four months before Christmas if yuh want real good black cake

my home name is gyal
with sugar diabetes
drinking bitter bush to cure it
but sneaking a lil cake on de side.

Sugar

My pancreas was fretful
and never did work well
the day it finally gave out
it ambushed my entire planet

from hibiscus to orange blossom
from insulin shock to
hospital bed
the thud of ripe mangoes falling in thick mud

from nutmeg blurred eyes
to dusty charred shell
from penicillin to lantus
the ripe photographs of my life escaped
through old boarded-up windows

my sugar house cracked and folded in on itself
part of my threshold gone forever
dear missing pancreas   I love you
you strange and unforgettable bastard.

Zuihitsu on Eating Poems

At fourteen
I learn the ways of poetry
how it enters your heart then hands full frame

it works its way down the torso then out of the mouth
that glorious undeveloped mouth that only knows chap stick and girlish giggles

a mouth unknown to beauty
still innocent to the delicious pineapple of a woman's kiss

at twenty
I fell out with my new husband of less than a year
my four-month-old son and I climbed into my mother's bed she held us
and read poems

Mom reads Gwendolyn Brooks   Georgia Douglas Johnson
she reads Derek Walcott   Léopold Senghor and Langston Hughes
something shifts at the magic of their songs

the husband calls and calls we do not answer
what holds me is this mystic doorway of words
and the rich hum of my mother's voice in the living room of these poems

a crop of words loop my heart there are
azaleas and hibiscus where the hurt
used to be

Hibiscus rosa
lowers blood sugar   lowers cholesterol
lowers blood pressure

prevents heart disease
its root soothes mucous membranes

hibiscus flowers are also known as Jamaican sorrel
as a child in Trinidad I drank sorrel
in Jamaica I drank sorrel and ate poems

I decorate my windows with pink azaleas and red hibiscus
place hibiscus at the front door for abundance

I eat poems for breakfast
sprinkle some on my honeydew melon
on my Inca red quinoa
I feed poems to my son he eats them
like heirloom tomatoes

later when he is gone I make murals of poems
each painted with the Bulgarian rose of tree bark
while the kettle hums I lure another string of words lithe like dragonflies
the wail of tribes ascending in the language of leaves.

Toco

The unfinished house in Toco
my father took me to the summer
I still loved him

walls still unhung he draped
a sheet so I could change into my swimsuit
his limbs bamboo slim

he made ginger lemonade
and sweetened it with ole talk
and fresh orange slices

the unfinished house in Toco
where later I waited
for his 1960s green DeSoto
to round the coast,

waited for a postcard
the wonder-of-the-world leaf
grew roots in my notebook,

I waited for the flared crowing of his voice
across water,
the bend of his arms around my neck
a ruby necklace to be worn.

Riding the World

My father had so many women
he stepped between their funk
riding the world   Mambo
Zouk   Soca   Chutney Bhangra

who could stop him his breath
thickening to paste
a caravan of limbs trailed behind him

a small room in his palm reserved for me
his river grew loud and deafening
long wounds on my mother's doorstep.

THAT AUGUST

Comets

My father draws a map
promises my mother the river
a mirror   pyramids
he grows her a lime tree   buys her a camel
and a white coat of lamb's hair

my mother sits on the steps of my father's house
her waist the size of his grandmother's gold bangle
he's given her this glowing gem for her twenty-fourth   birthday

under my mother's floral waistband
my twin brother and I keep ourselves secret
we read tea leaves to decide who will tell

my mother is the canvas
upon which father paints his ark
father is a rocket jet's mother's heart

when moonlight softens the earth
they walk in each other's footsteps

my twin and I become comets
we lance them
we lance them apart.

Twin Brother Speaks / 1950

Three nights my twin brother planned our escape
it's time to go now, he whispered
he said it so low Mammie did not hear him

be quick, he said reaching for his hat
throwing me his raincoat
he moved toward the door

come now, the hammock of his arms beckoning
I'm not ready, I said
he handed me the soft bread of his lips

the cool metal of his teeth   *sell it*
if you ever need shelter
then he was gone.

That August

Did you know my mother
slight slip of a girl
hips a wooden washboard
hair a runaway kite

father did you know my mother
her half-Indian eyes bright as fireflies
her black majestic rain of hair
it was her flaming pride
did you know

a sharp muscular cry hurls the night
blood a red hat
knitted to braids and bone

news climbed the town like wildfire
father did you know my mother then
slight slip of a girl
garnets for eyes
mouth a cracked earth exploding.

Birthmark

Mother to twin daughter / 1950

You are my oar   pillar   half

my boat   looking glass   wings

you are my straw broom   promise

promise me now   my girl

you are my secret   confession

promise   kiss me

girl   crack red dirt road   sting   bite   roar

you are my   village   scream   breath   not clear   fire

daughter   earth my   gazelle   you are my stain

you are   my   shame

my   brave sunrise   moonflower

moan   scream   sing   howl   salmon   butterfly

blue   root

you are   gospel   word   tree   black bark

        cry   serenade   break the night flap

fill my vein   light the city   crystal-tail mermaid.

Loan

Mother to twin son / 1950

Blue boy   never had no name

   boy   is all

got five names for twin girl   none for twin boy

already got a boy   don't need no more mouth to feed

hell   damn   look what you did city bus hit us one Friday

ride me until   my boy blue   he still

             why you go and do that   city bus

twin boy   he mine   twin boy gone now   my lil soldier

my shame   sin   lord   I   pay

         bus steal my womb   rip—   my—

Friday evening   five o clock   city bus

bus   wound   pierce   stole my boy

twin boy   you are   are you   my blessing

old people say plenty trouble if owl   sit on yuh windowsill

                                        plenty cry yuh see

that owl come too   bring

bring big green   city bus

                steal boy

                        steal dust from womb

boy   stillborn   he my

                cocoon   village   breath   wait for me   sweet   boy

promise

    kiss me   don't   go

bye soldier   tree trunk

bus crush   womb to spice   nutmeg   mauby   bitter bark

hold my hands   you are my—

    don't   go—   baby boy

forgive me   love boy   don't

go   no

loan   me to you one more day

you are my   face   shield   rosary   you are

my blessing   please   stay   your breath like far away

hold my hand shadow   weave a dream   in me.

I NAME GYAL

Who See She

Who see she
torn strip ah banana leaf
breadfruit tree lashing galvanize on top house
who hear she laughing hard
loud for no reason
the whole house smelling nice
just from the one small piece ah salt fish
grandma put in the pot   who see she

dancing in rain under mango tree
adding two spoon ah vanilla essence
and more sugar to the cassava pone
who see she toting bucket on she head
the spilling water wetting up the lil breast
she just get

who see she
singing hymns so sweetly
she eight-year-old hands folded with prayer
bare feet skipping through she childhood town
who see she
Arima gyal who knew to sing
braids long black mist slapping wind.

Leaving Trinidad

I, stumbling down the stairs
of Port-of-Spain general hospital
into the broad and yellow light

I wanted to take the stairs back up three at a time
grab my mother out of her sick bed and beg
don't let me leave you, Mammie
don't make me go

bless Uncle Alvin
telling me to be a good girl
to listen to Aunt Ena,
America, that's not so bad;

yuh not a pretty girl   but yuh smart
smarter than all dem boys put together;
yuh brain big and yuh mouth bigger

make yuh old Uncle proud
my body stalled with sobs
I could barely hear anything.

Gone

We walked wordless
along the tarmac
to the waiting airplane
nineteen sixty-four my small gloved hand
clasped in my father's bare brown hands
at the top of the stairs I looked back
to wave one last time
his limbs long and departing
in the bright Trinidad sun

my world already turned from me.

Limes for the Journey

For my father

The last time I saw my father   standing in Aunt Girlie's yard
he looked aged and senile   he was drunk and peeing
on the eggplants in her vegetable garden
he told me his lover was not sexing him enough

this crazy stranger
who once braided my hair and   took me to church

         not even the reverence of sleep could quell this expanding ache

once my father brought his first crop of mangoes to my first grade class
they were crimson and delicious as my father's kiss

months later
the furniture of his mouth gone
eyes bloodied and slow moving
he carried the smell of stale lodging in his skin

        my hands   my hands

  they carry your fear   the broken slats   that house your dreams

the remnants of your kiss like mother's milk makes a pale line around my
   mouth
there is life after malt liquor

each season mangoes unfold their zippered skin
there is praise in your long neglected arms

dad

        If   I could forget the uselessness of that year

your heart a slight bird
burying its head in the stern crack of your shame—-

one cruel leaf escapes my heart

                        I'm obsessed with rage
        how far does one have to walk to find forgiveness
you pick limes from your small laden tree
and even though I tell you   I cannot take them on the plane
you sort the good ones the ones with perfect stems
the ones without spots and worms

you pack   and pack them in a bright yellow box with gold trim

here daughter
something for your journey   the small fruit   heavy   in the box.

I Name Gyal 2

November 1, 1964

Day of the dead
Gyal take flight from planet hummingbird
ibeji dauter born of ibeji mother
gyal reach America

Tanty Ena meet gyal at Kennedy airport

in the maroon chevy nova
she bring a long brown coat with fur lining

she bring gloves boots and fur hat
gyal eh like dem tings
lord they too big and fluffy
gyal prefer she bright island clothes and she trini dialect

next day gyal step in the school big and important
wearing she island colors proud   proud
I name gyal, she beams
the chiren laugh loud at she accent

The Sea at Marabella

Southern coast of Trinidad

I want the pound of ocean
by the sea in Marabella

I want my wooly fat braids
tied to flying ribbons flapping like bird wings

I want my stick thin legs
running after cousin Villma's bike

begging for a ride
mouth filled with salt air and nutty sand

I want the loose butts of old women
falling out of their too-small swimsuits

their eyes halfway hidden
under the rims of big panama hats

their french creole
spicing up the dead jellyfish thick air

I want to churn the wooden ice cream freezer
while the boys pack it with salt and ice

I want my Trinidad
her chest a finely sculpted bamboo bowl

her shoulders the bright jawbone of God
I want to feel the sting of hot sand

the pound of ocean
from my Marabella sea.

Independence Day

Mom arrived in New York City
a day before July fourth
one year since I last saw her

in her travel bag a small red bible
a handful of caraili bush for sugar diabetes
and painful cramps   a sou-sou book
and a red solo

later in bed I hugged Mammie tight tight
we talked all night, then she said chile
I missed the roar ah yuh big mouth most

girl, I din tell plenty people I was going away yuh kno
din want nobody to put goat mouth on me
and then I never reach America

we fell apart with crazy laughter

Poodles and Sour Cream

I am the third generation of daughters
whose mother worked as a domestic
in that Great Neck house of poodles and sour cream
girls younger than me
called my mother by a nickname

Genie, what's for breakfast
Genie, wash my hair
Genie, take my bike out
Genie, get my boots off

my mother who raised me to call elders
tanty, uncle, granny related or not
Tanty Evelyn, Tanty Vida, Uncle Dadoo, Uncle Horatio
even the bum with the limp was called Mister Broke-up-foot

in that cold New York house
my mother spent three years eating mashed potatoes
and sour cream doing sleep-in work
waiting for she green card to come

and every night crying for she beloved daughter
she could not care for while raising the white lady chiren.

I Name Gyal 3

My home name is gyal
I remember who I am braided gyal
drinking cocoa tea eating fry bake

I make sardines in onion stew
just like Mammie teach me
I remember who I am

I remember to say paliwal, not best friend

remember to say bodi, not string beans
remember to say melongen, not eggplant

zaboca, not avocado
remember to say, she bold face, fast an out-ah-place
remember I more bold than she

everybody say, so long you in America
you still have accent
I am the daughter of Elma and Roy
I name gyal, I say.

My Eyes So Much Like Hers

We visit the bird woman
in that dark Brooklyn apartment

on the table coils of brown rubber
gauze and white gloves

on the stove water boils
in a chipped blue pot

there in a tissue
my mother breaks her good Christian vow

that rainy Monday
my baby was taken

you must have college
mother says

her lips heavy with few words
a sure future brims in her eyes

and the no good boyfriend
gone off to college

dissecting a frog   playing soccer
the new girl in his arms

when did you lose your wide eyes

tears don't fill the empty
three times he calls

I come back to his mocking voice
his talk dirty like swamp water

the long distance phone lines
my broken umbilical cord

mom brings me chicken soup
I cannot look at her face
my eyes so much like hers.

Knitting Lesson

My twentieth year returns
the embryos I threw away like birdseed
waits at my door
in the kitchen my son pours coffee at the breakfast table
I knit worlds together
using tears and umbilical cords to make poems

Things I Do in the Dark

After June Jordan

this crying
praying
sweet fondling
reaching for milk drained breasts
all I find are dry stalks
this crude wire
this crooked strut

this wooden fish
this dried smoke
this marigold wreath
this pink rose quartz
this holy water
these are things I do in the dark

this clawing of self
this crying   hurting
praying   paying ghosts
this crude gauze mouth
this kneading of flesh to make whole again

these are things I do in the dark
this piecing together
this mauve body
this flat rubber heart

and where did I go
where did I go

reaching for that fly yellow-girl
where did I go
this spirit talk
spirit talk   talking   taking
hurricane route of middle passage

talking in the dark   praying
tying the head in white cotton
circling the hips with red beads
calling calling the dead
calling Chango Oya

mama where did I go
this midwife
this bird walk
this meteor
this shell reader
sweet bush beater

this white candle   this cowrie shell
tarot cards   this peacock feather
this cigar
white veil
praying in the dirt
flirting with the dance.

Hush the Call of Names

This is the year we hush
the call of names
our dead are stars
they have outlasted
this tincture of dried wreaths

let the dead release their porcelain confessions
their words a saffron tapestry
woven with the joys of its own geography
give them back their magic

in this coming season of colored leaves
our lives hum with true abundance

listen   listen   hush
cease the call of names
give the dead back their beauty
let their eyes return like agates

let their noise in this room be poems
be topaz
be blue iris
a cup of hibiscus tea

and from this moment
lift your head for signs of life
and from this moment
let us sing   let us sing
let us begin again.

SPELL

Worship

She eats smoked almonds
slowly   from my fingers
licks the pink Himalayan salt
from the bend of my palm
this is how worship begins.

Husband

What lovely star
caused your hand to fall across my waist

your fingers whistled
through the streets of my December hair
      your talk lowered me to the dance floor
      each line punctured with longing
until hallelujah
I led her to my queen bed
      at the brightest corner of the room
      days later I call her husband.

Blue Heart Zuihitsu

Once we moved in my lover would wake in the middle of the night saying
babe my back is itching
I would brush her back   until she moaned and slept against the sloped howl
    of night

this afternoon after the mammogram my breast still stings from the shit of a
    machine
named after a woman   Imagine that
no woman would create a contraption that could cause other women such pain

I walked through the farmer's market along Adam Clayton Powell Plaza   the
    slight
pungent smell of fresh chard   rosemary   rhubarb   tickled my nostrils   I
    moved
in closer to soothe my ache

South of London
I walked down Eddy Grant's Electric Avenue, pass Brockwell Park
memories of Jay Day Cannabis festival still hung in the trees
1960s tie dye head wraps   cowrie earrings   floral bell bottom jeans

In Brixton they recognize my Trini right away   Scotch bonnet
peppers and jerk sauce on my tongue   my mouth tears into an East Indian
    mango

    she said   she *gets angry when I'm sick—*

    said   she *wants me to put on my big girl panties (the ones I buy in bulk at
    Duane
Reade) and take care of my shit—*

last night she tore my skin   that's right tore my skin
she should have worn a muzzle for this vacation
in the water was a mirror   I saw the bruise of her words take
    shape   claws   then   knives
bruised my small black—

two days of silence followed   two days of silence

then my lover said
I don't really get angry
I get scared   can you forgive me
one
more
time   forgive—

I passed the lake   stood under the blueberry grove of trees

    hearts of berries stained the ground a deep blue

forgive me
she says

I tore my skin

    felt it open
exposed the dumb gnarled pulp

finally my heart turned
miss mermaid has weeds in her tail
there are adjectives up for sale

did I tell you I was a twin

    I cannot remember which self loved her so much
everyday   less   less

less everyday less   every
day   love her

less

        I remember the year I took my girl out for an exotic father's day
        dinner
             she was the daddy of our house then
the next year for father's day   I made a Trinidadian pelau   with crab lobster
  and pigeon peas

I wanted to make it an annual tradition—

scallions mint leaves   bits of mango chutney   rice in coconut milk   and for
  desert
ginger watermelon with raw honey on top

I served it on our living room floor clad in bare feet   half an orange bugle
  beaded
Sari   and my blue-fish-eyed bindi

—on the kitchen counter

   the glass table
the bathroom floor   holy god

praise tenderness
the sickle moon of her
bent against the bedside lamp

still stops my heart.

Spell

I carry my big-up self to Trinidad
hoping the sea water could wash way
the bitter taste of mal yeux blight
that not so good woman leave in my house

a nasty wind blow in my face when I reach Tunapuna
fish market it nearly make me faint
I rush off the damn put-put taxi and ask the woman
in the pretty guava sari and the blue henna painted hands

how much it does cost to light a white candle
for broken hearts here
she look at me good and with a serious face she say
candles eh go help yuh nah missy but here what and follow me good

get a brasso tin and put yuh private business in it
bury it on the first river bank yuh see
take two rum and wine yuh waist like it ha spring
for three days drink tea bag black no coffee

take two sea bath it go cut that mal yeux blight
I giving yuh two cigar light one for every sea bath
I go give yuh a small bag ah vetivee grass
hang it round yuh neck

then guava say   *six hundred miss-lady*
six hundred for what
I is the cheapest round here ask anybody

I don't want to fight this early morning
miss-lady just pay me my money
cash only nocreditcardamericanexpress
noting like that just cash

four weeks pass and nothing working
the veti making me sneeze
the spring in my waist so rusty it break
and the rum giving me bad feeling

to tell the truth I fraid sea water
and I was hoping to work half the spell
cause half the heart ready
the other half still pending.

I Name Gyal 4

I name gyal
I am the daughter I always wanted
I grow tropical crotons in my kitchen

long crimson and yellow stems
that look like they can dance
I name gyal

I got tall orange and red balisier in my bedroom
their bright mouths red as Shango's shout
my straw mat is strewn with guavas purple cowry shells and Oya candles

I remember who I am   my home name is gyal
my study is wild with stray ferns
Boston, Jamaican, English and stink Mexican marigolds

I rise at five start my dinner
a pot of curry chicken and rice on the stove
fresh corn from the yard

my home name is gyal
in summer I plant wild pumpkin vine and blue dasheen
lay sorrel in the yard to dry

sweeten ginger beer with molasses
churn Guinness stout into ice cream
invite friends, play reggae and soca loud

I am my own midwife, I birth myself
the daughter I always wanted
I am my best self   braided gyal
drinking cocoa tea.

After the Storm

She grew so beautiful it was hard to find the cracks.

Tools

A woman's body has everything in it
to save her life

if you must
use your legs as raft

heel as hammer
teeth as machete

monthly blood as healing salve
milk for building

breasts as shelter
learn to breathe

use your locks to suture every wound
learn to scream

learn to scream
learn to speak

learn to live
within the smallest muscle of your heart.

In This Pure Light

Zuihitsu for a son

1.

October 2008

We are in the hospital waiting room at
University of California in San Francisco
my son is about to have a kidney transplant
my daughter-in-law is the donor

    a dear friend gives my daughter-in-law a silver necklace
from it hangs three pearl shaped hearts   for love   strength   and hope
I ask to wear the necklace during surgery

2.

November 1970

Dear son
On this joyous morning   sheets still smell of birth
our newborn inheritance between us
still an unburned bride my body blooms
become   river boat village grave
your small mouth sewn to my blue flesh   glows

your twin brother
gone to meet the breath of God   waiting in that field of light

son
   you are my pillar tree wealth straw-broom looking glass   wings scream
   temple
fire
   break the night   light the city   love

                         does the organ of the heart shiver in this pure light
or does the light shiver in the presence of the heart

3.

I so want love
   can this dyke-mama body absorb all that light

bombastic red
I rouge my mouth

ease out the door
my tightest dress   the green brocade
piano plays

4.

June 1985

The house on Merrick Boulevard
my son's dad tells him I am a lesbian

he screams and cries roars his rage
earth hums with ache
one snapped tree broken at its center
he is fifteen   my son a kiss slips from my palm

I fear this death more than I fear my own

pain has slimmed me

the next few years I grow a Judas body   a false tongue
my eyes a watercraft for the Gods
        my son grows narrow in the damp of boyhood
           the questions of his body a crooked dirt road
much later he becomes a spell maker
        I adore his sensitive words

5.

Last night on the phone my son hums me one of his new tunes
tells me   *I always knew I'd be a rapper of positive thoughts*
he tells me   *I love my grandmother but when she tried to pray my hip hop*
  dreams
away
I would repeat in my head I will have my music I will have my music
  someday I
will I will

his body became a temple for hip hop

When I found out my son was a diabetic

I wished to make his curse mine   inside I burned with blue shame   I had
  given him bad
sugar
I had given him my diabetes

four needles	four shots of insulin
four shots of insulin	a handful of pills
that's what it takes to make my body work each day	four Peri exchanges

                           that's what it takes for my son's body

to work each day

                   Mother's day 1999
                   my son calls to say
                   he needs a kidney

6.

That night I beg God to give me the burden   forgive my sins
is it because I love a woman
God
I make a pact
God
I swear I will—

7.

there's blood on my knees
I paint my face holy
the color of white apple blossoms   I make another pact with God

8.

On the flight from Brooklyn to Oakland   I pray and pray
my son is getting sicker   I don't know how to comfort him/me

             My grandson David   meets me at the airport
          he hops on one leg all the way to the baggage carousel

I'm gonna give Malik my kidney   he says
I will   I   will   I'm not scared ah nothin—
he is eight

We go directly to the hospital my son is asleep
I sit at his bedside and wait
two A.M. the phone rings   my girl is on the line
how did the test results go   she asks
                              we are quiet for a long time

My son stirs
I drop the phone   I hug my child   I hold his hand in mine   kiss him
rub his head   squeeze him   squeeze him
until he says
ouch   ouch   ouch   ma

B. B. King's Revival

For Malik Izaak

I watched him build a wall
watched him build a revival tent
my son with his own breath

a bobblehead nodder
his eyes did amaze me   the color
espresso with a glob of cream

his arms did amaze me   flex point
a black maestro the Itzhak Perlman
he's middle named for

that curled-Trini mouth
wild almost menacing
make-some-noise-some-muther-fuckin-
noise-we-in-new-york

his voice did amaze me
but it was the ones who screamed
I watched them become cartoonish and off kilter

voice thin and whiny
hollow as bajan coins
I watched my son imbue them

with his hip hop moonshine
they drunk holy rollers
who had just received the spirit

his flock hip hop pilgrims
rising up to touch him
he   my boy revival preacher.

ARRIVAL

The Red Bible

You try on your mother's tan and brown shoes
she bought on her trip to Rome
you keep the lime-green ribbon from her suitcase
her aqua and white suit for Irma
red Bible with her name in gold for Malik
navy-blue linen blazer for Ceni
will it fit
her red and white crochet quilt for Deisha
will she like it
you sort clothing for the Salvation Army
you go back to that pile and take things out
her crème car coat for Donna
it fits perfect
you wear her delicate white Fossil watch
a present from her grandson
you keep her broken glasses use it for reading
you find her nurses pin and cap with the black stripe
Zinzi offers to put some furniture on eBay or is it craigslist
you keep her bras, socks, slippers, flannel nightgowns
you will need her to keep warm this winter.

Arrival

An elegy

on the day I arrive my best friend Rodlyn will wake early and sweep the drain
in front   she little trinket shop   she will put all the blue sequined bracelets
and silver scarves up front   she knows I will try them on first
blue green yellow   then pink

Mom will peel a few grapefruits   those huge pink-skinned ones
        they sweeter than them   pale   wash-out whitey ones yuh know
that's her way to point up her feelings for white folks   not too veiled   not
    too brash

she will fix my favorite peanut punch add a dash of rum   the rum really for
    she
but she go pretend it for me

            my father will try to put his arms around her   she will
            say   *look   leave meh alone yes   mister*
            she will take a few sips of the peanut punch then get back to her
hat making   peacock blue and yellow felt bound by a black shiny crushed
    velvet band

my father will put on coffee   he will sit on the front porch   chin in right
    hand and greet
every big bottom women walking by

once I get settled mom will come to my room and present me with my felt and
    velvet hat
amid tears and kisses she will say

what took you so long to come   Cheryl   I missed yuh   everyday   missed yuh oh
God

she will say   *how's   Malik meh darling boy*
and yuh lady-friend Ceni   yuh still wid she and Cheryl why yuh wearing blue eye
shadow
wha kinda color is that
who tell yuh it pretty
yuh didn't find de right color for yuh pretty dark complexion in de store
but is not everything them thief selling for yuh to buy   yuh know gyal

    I thought I   teach you better
anyway never mind all that   I have so much to tell yuh lord

Cheryl yuh see your father   that man eh change.

Roy

For my father

All he had left:
his tamarind polished limbs
gaps between the squares of his teeth

the sea is a collector of dreams
what I would not give for his browning bark of fingers
the lives between those sequined bones
his garnet and silver wedding ring metal beaten flat

what I would not give for the selfish dust
in his laughter
the precious copper of his tongue clacking

morning   the gone moon
picks at these blue-cadmium bones
my porcelain beak of body rises
I become window
frame.

Moonflower

In four weeks mom you will be dead four years
what more shall I make of your secrets and the dried flower petals
left in the pocket of your good dress

once the full moon opened my father's palm
released his umber-brown rage
on my eighth birthday daddy twisted my step mother's arm
right in front of me
she howled in pain then sent me to the store

chocolate ice cream
she said   *get chocolate in a cone   keep the change   keep your dress clean*
your mother wants you to keep your dress clean

later when she tucked me in bed she whispered
never marry   never marry   never marry a man   afraid of his own face

back at home
when I told mom
she became an open bible
a Psalm of David   she became Psalm 101.3
                              I will see no wicked thing before mine eyes:
she became a crack in the back door
her family geography   their dialect of sorrow
she became the bearer of her mother's secrets and her mother and her
mother before her
I want to scatter mother of pearl upon the stunned earth
somewhere a daughter pines for her mother
her mother a steep hill wired with ghosts

what
shall
I
make
of your secrets
and the dried flower petals
left in the pocket of your good dress

my father's cigarette lights the small bedroom

    I imagine a heavy heart growing inside
day smells of magic the vice of dawn moans like djembe drum.

remember when joy lingered

    mom's breast is weeping
the baby's receiving blanket smells of stale seaweed
mom wants the earth to echo cries of her blue newborn son

                womb a shattered cup sits on its rusted frame

with his baby boy gone dad moves on
he turns to the stout woman in the tight red dress

mom tends her citrine-yellow dahlias and her plump baby girl
her arms lean stalks of sugar cane

daddy brings a basket of goldenrod mangoes to my first grade class   we smell
    the hot
road and the sea salt in them   soon the school song freezes in our mouths and
    our voices
go astray   we taste the sap and sugar fruit warm like breast milk
high in our summer mouths

daddy I was hoping to make you a garland of seaweeds for your gleaming
   neck   a burlap
sack of dried fruit

I am my father's daughter   restless
with no August breeze   I   become a borrowed day

mom loves extra high heels   a milliner who make hats by the midnight
breath of her oil lamp
at fifteen
I sneak into my mother's closet and wear her leather boots and expensive
dresses to school

she becomes a deep throat brass band

quiet, please
grandmother pleads in her soft French-patois
       I float in and out of the music of her breath
       the way I float on my mom's back at the beach

on Sundays our kitchen smells like bok choy and ginger-salmon
mom sets the table for just us two
she recites her poems loudly   sun following her waistline around the room
her body a pulpit   her mouth calls to ecru-blue mountains
calls balisier   bacchanal and wayward tree

Once I placed a bunch of red and orange hibiscus blossoms on mom's night
   stand
I wanted her to observe the delicate way they broke skin
pushing ever so slightly into
the vortex of the room

             mom held her/my secrets deep in the ruby socket of her heart

   I will not forget the amethyst-blue corridors of your voice mother
your burnt-sienna fingers on my back like guitar strings

four years of missing you has made the small delicate bones of my spine into a
  church

    last night in my dream I tried to call you
what I wanted to say—
to say was—

    what kind of birthday cake would you like this year

    remember the year I bought
you a strawberry cheesecake   laughter slid off your jasper-brown skin

all night it rains
in the morning my forehead flush to the window
                        mom holds something out to me
a braid of moonflowers
and her arms.

FEB - - 2018